A CHRISTIAN HANDBOOK
FOR
DEFENDING THE FAITH

ROBERT A. MOREY

A CHRISTIAN HANDBOOK

FOR

DEFENDING THE FAITH

by
Robert A. Morey

Presbyterian and Reformed Publishing Company
Phillipsburg, New Jersey 08865

ISBN 0-87552-336-6

Printed in the United States of America

Dr. Morey received his B.A. in philosophy from Covenant College, a M.Div. and D.Min. from Westminster Theological Seminary. He has also written:
The Bible and Drug Abuse
The Dooyeweerdian Concept of the Word of God
The Saving Work of Christ
How to Answer a Jehovah's Witness
Reincarnation and Christianity
The Worship of God
Is Sunday the Christian Sabbath?
An Examination of Exclusive Psalmody

CONTENTS

INTRODUCTION

Christian apologetics is not the art of apologizing for being a Christian. Neither is it a special calling reserved only for a few Christian "intellectuals." Rather, it is an activity in which all Christians should be engaged in the normal course of their day to day witnessing for Christ in a world of unbelievers. All Christians have been commissioned by Christ and empowered by the Holy Spirit to be Christ's witness bearers (Matt. 28:19, 20; Acts 1:8). And one very vital and important aspect of witness bearing is the task of apologetics.

God's vision of what every Christian should be doing includes apologetics. Just as God envisions every believer as being "competent to counsel," even so He envisions every believer as being "competent to defend the Faith" (Jude 3). The average believer must not rob himself or herself of the joyous task of apologetics by assuming that it is best to let "clerical George" do it. *All* Christians are called to this task. When this truth finally dawns upon the 20th century church, perhaps we shall recapture the aggressiveness of the Protestant Reformation.

While there are many fine books on apologetics, few of them are simple enough for the average high school or college student. And when you try to find something for the businessman or housewife, you run into great difficulty. It is to this need that this small monograph is directed in the hope that it will introduce the average Christian to the subject of apologetics and, at the same time, serve as a catalyst to spur him on to do further research on the subject.

The first thing we should observe is that apologetics involves two different kinds of activities:

1. The *defensive* work of the believer is to defend the faith when it is attacked (Jude 3). The apostle Peter also states that our defense of the faith should not be sloppy but it should be an intelligent reply (I Peter 3:15).
   Example: A Dr. White has made a public attack on Christianity. He claims that Christianity is the cause behind the present ecological crisis. According to

1

him, Christianity breeds disrespect for the environment and leads to the wanton destruction of the earth. Pollution is the result of the acceptance of Christian beliefs. This is a deliberate attack on the Christian faith.[1] In defense of Christianity, Dr. Francis Schaeffer accepted Dr. White's challenge and has refuted his charges in a book.[2] In this work, Schaeffer demonstrates that biblical Christianity is not to blame for causing pollution.

2. The *offensive* work of the believer is to demonstrate that the non-Christian philosophies and religions are false and that only Christianity answers the ultimate questions of life.

Example: After Dr. White attacked Christianity by laying the blame for pollution on it, he then stated that the only way to deal with the crisis is to embrace the religions of the East and, in particular, the doctrine of pantheism. According to him, only by turning to Eastern religions such as Zen-Buddhism can we solve the present ecological problems.

Dr. Schaeffer also accepted this challenge and demonstrates in his book on pollution that the Eastern religions do not and, indeed, cannot give a sufficient basis upon which to deal with the present environmental crisis. Dr. Schaeffer goes on to prove that only Christianity can provide a true basis for working out the environmental problems.

Thus Dr. Schaeffer does two things in his book. He *defends* Christianity and *defeats* the non-Christian philosophy of Dr. White. Schaeffer is both negative and positive in his apologetics.

Our goals in this study on apologetics are:

1. To survey briefly the many ways in which the various non-Christian systems or world-and-life views fail.

2. To put forth the different ways in which the Christian can challenge and refute non-Christian systems of thought.

3. To set forth several illustrations of how the Christian world-and-life view can be developed in various areas of life.

---

1. Lynn White, Jr., "The Historical Roots of our Ecological Crisis." *Science,* vol. 155, pp. 1203-1207, 10 March 1967.
2. Francis A. Schaeffer, *Pollution and the Death of Man: The Christian View of Ecology,* Tyndale House Publishers, Wheaton, Ill. 1970.

PART ONE

THE PREPARATION OF THE LIFE

But sanctify Christ as Lord in your hearts, always being ready to make a defense to every man who asks you to give an account for the hope that is in you, yet with gentleness and reverence; having a good conscience (I Peter 3:15-16).

In the above passage we find not only the call to do apologetics but also the necessary preparation which apologetics requires, for we are told to "sanctify Christ as Lord" in our hearts *before* we can "make a defense."

The sanctifying of Christ as Lord involves two things.

I. *Receiving Christ as the Lord of your life in terms of salvation.* In order to do Christian apologetics you must be a *bona fide* Christian. The issue of personal salvation is very important in apologetics for several reasons.

First, if the apologist is not saved, the Holy Spirit will not empower his witness with true boldness. Apologetics is then reduced to a mere intellectual debate. It becomes composed of mere words and will not be given or received "in power and in the Holy Spirit and with full conviction" (I Thess. 1:5).

Second, the unregenerate apologist stands a good chance of being "converted" to the non-Christian position. Too many young people become excited about apologetics and end up losing their faith because their faith was actually an empty profession (I John 2:19).

Let the reader stop and ask himself, "Have I ever really received Jesus Christ as my own personal Lord and Savior? Do I see and do others see in my life definite clear-cut evidence that I am born again?" Self-examination is a biblical responsibility which is an absolute necessity for apologetics (II Cor. 13:5).

3

II. Sanctifying Christ as Lord also involves *obeying Christ as the Lord of your life in terms of holiness*. Without holiness of life, the Christian will not be effective in witnessing no matter how "intellectual" or "airtight" his apologetics may be.

Obeying Christ as Lord in the Christian life involves several things.

A. The Christian must deal with his own personal sins. He must not hide or rationalize them away. He must repent of and confess his sins or he will not prosper in witnessing (Prov. 28:13; I John 1:9).

It is very important that the apologist should never engage in defending the faith until he has confessed his sins afresh to God. There must not be a single conscious controversy between the apologist and God because He will not hear you if sin is retained in the heart (Ps. 66:18).

B. The Christian who would do apologetics must consistently read the Scriptures, and constantly test his ideas by biblical truth in order to grow personally and to be guided in the ways of God.

C. The importance of prayer cannot be overstressed. The prayerless Christian is the powerless apologist. Not only must you pray before you witness, but during and after the witness, prayer should be constantly ascending to God. It is good to ask God quickly for wisdom when handling any difficult questions (James 1:5-8).

If you are engaged in a group effort at apologetics where any of the brothers or sisters are speaking, then constant prayer must be made for them while they present the Christian position. If they are not supported by prayer, it is not likely that many true conversions will follow.

D. There must be the preparation of a proper attitude before the believer can engage in apologetics. The apostle Peter said to defend the faith "with gentleness and reverence." Or, as Paul in II Timothy 2:23-26 states, "But refuse foolish and ignorant speculations, knowing that they produce quarrels. And the Lord's bond-servant must not be quarrelsome, but be kind to all, able to teach, patient when wronged, with gentleness correcting those who are in opposition, if perhaps God may grant them repentance leading to the knowledge of the truth, and they may come to their senses and escape from the snare of the devil, having been held captive by him to do his will."

The Christian must deal with the problem of pride because "God is opposed to the proud, but gives grace to the humble" (James 4:6). If the unbeliever senses that you are filled with contempt or an air of superiority, he will not listen to you.

E. Lastly, the apostle Peter also points out the necessity of a "good conscience." A good conscience is a clear conscience void of offense toward God or man (Acts 24:16). There cannot be any unresolved conflicts between you and God or between you and others. Clear your conscience by following the procedure laid out in Matthew 18:15-19 or Matthew 5:23-24. Seek to maintain a good conscience at all times. Boldness before others is rooted in maintaining a good conscience.

PART TWO

THE IMPORTANT QUESTIONS

There are two major schools of apologetics: Presuppositional and Evidential.
 I. *What they have in common:* The same *goals.*
   Both schools want to defend Christianity, to refute the non-Christian systems and to demonstrate that Christianity is the only valid way of living and believing.
 II. Where they differ: They differ as to the *methods* they employ to achieve the same goals. Simply put: *The Presuppositionalists argue from "presuppositions." The Evidentialists argue from "evidences."*
 III. Clarification by way of diagram #1
   There are two ways to sink a ship: torpedo it from below or blow it to pieces with guns from above.

Non-Christian Ship   Evidentialistic Ship

Evidentialists, attacking from above, destroy non-Christian concepts (science, reason, personal experience, etc.) Presuppositionalists, attacking from below, will destroy the non-Christian presuppositions.

Diagram 1   Presuppositionalist Sub

6

The evidentialist will defend the Christian position and defeat the non-Christian system of thought by "facts" drawn from

    A. Science (history, geology, etc.)

    B. Reason (logic, common sense, etc.)

    C. Personal experience (conversion, miracles, etc.)

The presuppositionalist will attack the non-Christian presuppositions as being inconsistent, non-livable, etc.

Now look at diagram #2, which explains and illustrates the questions or challenges which can be put to any system of thought.

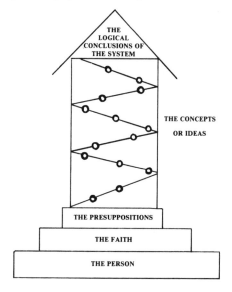

Diagram 2

1. The *person* is the foundation of any system, for the nature of the person determines the precepts. Who and what we are determines who and what we can know or understand. Too often we forget that we are dealing with a *person* and not just with a position. The nature of the person determines our methods in apologetics.

2. The *faith* which underlies the presuppositions needs to be examined, for at the bottom of every system there is faith.

3. We must examine the *presuppositions* which underlie a system and from which the concepts are developed.

4. Next comes the *individual concepts* or *ideas* which make up the bulk or substance of the system.

7

5. In the last section we come to the *logical conclusion* of the system, for if we are consistent, the system will take us somewhere. Where it will take us is the crucial question.

Now that we have examined the diagram in general, let us apply it to typical non-Christian systems of thought.

The following are challenging questions which we have a right to apply to any system of thought. Thus they should be posed to each section of any non-Christian system of thought.

IV. Questions concerning the *person* who holds the position.

A. *Aren't we dealing with someone created in God's image?*

1. This question deals with our attitude towards non-Christians. We should view them in love as being very important and significant to us because they are image-bearers.

Example: Why are so many non-Christians converted at L'Abri? Is it only because of the tremendous intellectual arguments presented there? Not really. Anyone who visits L'Abri soon discovers that it is also the *love* manifested and demonstrated at L'Abri that wins the hearts of many non-Christians. People are treated in the light that although the image of God in man was corrupted by Adam's fall into sin, it was not totally eradicated. Thus man is not an animal or a machine but is still God's image-bearer. We must view and treat all men in the light of this truth.

2. This question reveals to us who they really are and what they know deep down in their heart of hearts. From Romans chapters one and two, we learn that all men know three immutable facts:

a. That God exists (Rom. 1:18-25). This they see from the *creation* around them.

b. That they are sinful creatures (Rom. 2:12-16). This they know by their *conscience* within them.

c. Even though all men know the above by virtue of the image of God within them, Romans 1:18 states that all men "suppress" or "hold down" the truth in unrighteousness. Because of sin, men will deny what they know in their heart of hearts.

B. *Aren't we dealing with someone who is totally depraved as a result of Adam's fall into sin and guilt?*

1. *Intellectually,* the non-Christian will reject and oppose biblical Christianity because his heart is darkened (Rom. 1:21) and his mind is blinded by Satan (II Cor. 4:4). Thus, non-Christians are spiritually incapable of understanding the truth (I Cor. 2:14). The gospel is

8

foolishness to them (I Cor. 1:18). They suppress the truth that is in their hearts (Rom. 1:18).

2. *Morally,* they are wedded to their sins and they really do not want to repent of their sins. Did not our Lord Himself give us this very realistic truth in John 3:19-20? "And this is the condemnation, that light is come into the world, and men loved darkness rather than light, because their deeds were evil. For every one that doeth evil hateth the light, neither cometh to the light, lest his deeds should be reproved."

   Example: In running a counseling center in Greenwich Village of New York City, we encountered many drug addicts. One young man named Josie was a sad example of the love of sin. When confronted with the gospel he responded by saying, "I refuse to become a Christian because it would mean that I would have to give up my sin and I *refuse* to do so!" He was a slave to his sin (John 8:36; Rom. 6:17).

3. *Volitionally,* without the new birth, they cannot see, enter or receive the kingdom of God (John 3:1-5; 6:44) for in their hearts they actually hate God (Rom. 1:30; 8:7; John 3:20).

   Example: The unregenerate's hatred of God is most visible when they curse using God's name whenever anything goes wrong. It is helpful at times to ask the unbeliever if he ever used God's name in vain. If truthful, he will answer in the affirmative. Then read Exodus 20:4-7 which shows that all sin is ultimately rooted in man's hatred of God.

4. *Sin renders man ethically insane or irrational.* Because of sin man will act at times just like a mindless unfeeling animal.

   Example: The biblical concept of man's depravity supplies us with the only way to understand the inhuman atrocities which Hitler committed against the Jews and which the Communists now perpetrate against the Christians.[3]

C. *Isn't the real problem moral and not intellectual?*

1. True faith will not come through argumentation (II Tim. 2:23-26).

2. There is more than enough evidence on every hand from every department of human experience and knowledge to demonstrate that Christianity is true. The light is shining and the music is playing but the non-Christian shuts his eyes and plugs his ears and

---

3. Richard Wurmbrand, *Underground Saints,* Logos International, Plainfield, N.J., 1968.

then pretends that there is neither light nor sound.
3. Because the basic problem is moral, our approach must be given in terms of a confrontation. We need to confront sinners lovingly with the fact of their sin and boldly and authoritatively to proclaim repentance and faith. We must never believe or act as though Christianity is just one option among many. It is God's *only* answer to man's moral dilemma.

D. *Shouldn't the gospel be our main subject?*
Apologetics may prepare the way for, accompany or follow the gospel, but never let apologetics displace the gospel. Too often apologetics becomes an "ego trip" because the apologist is more concerned with winning the argument than with winning the person.

V. Questions concerning the *faith* which underlies the presuppositions.

A. *Does this faith have any grounds in the world around us or in the nature of man himself? Is it subjective in its content as well as in its commitment?*
The faith of the non-Christian is externally and internally groundless. They are the ones who leap into the dark. Some, like Kierkegaard, have admitted this.
Example: The 20th century abounds with atheistic humanists who have a utopian faith about man's future. On every newsstand there are humanistic utopian science-fiction books which picture man as evolving into a love-filled creature who no longer makes war and where all mankind lives as one family without greed, crime, hatred or selfishness. There is manifestly no evidence for such utopian hopes in (1) man's nature or (2) in the history of the world.

B. *Isn't this faith ethically directed?*
1. We must emphasize that there is no neutrality—not even in science. Objectivity is a myth.[4]
2. Some anti-Christian concepts are believed simply because they are anti-Christian.

Example: Some scientists openly admit that they believe in the theory of evolution because *the only alternative is creation.* They admit that evolution as a theory has never been proven and that there is much evidence against it. Mathematically, Polini and others have proven that evolution is impossible. The M.I.T. computers have confirmed this to be true. Given up to six billion

---

4. Gordon H. Clark, *The Philosophy of Science and Belief in God,* The Craig Press, Nutley, N.J., 1964.

10

years, chance, and matter—what is the probability that the complex earth which now exists could have evolved to its present state by pure chance? The mathematical answer is zero probability.

Here is one illustration which Polini developed to demonstrate the problem the evolutionists have to deal with. Imagine that as you travel into Wales by train, you see at the border on a hillside the words—"Welcome to Wales"—arranged out of white stones. It is more probable, statistically speaking, for those by stones by chance to pop out of the earth by themselves, by chance to develop a white exterior, by chance to roll together and spell out the words "Welcome to Wales" than it is for the evolutionary theory to be true.

VI. Questions concerning the *presuppositions*.
   A. *What are your presuppositions—assumptions—starting points?*
      Example: You meet a non-Christian who tells you, "I do not believe that Jesus arose bodily from the grave." It is obvious that the real problem behind this man's rejection of Christ's resurrection is his presuppositions. When you examine his presuppositions you find out *why* he rejects the resurrection.

      Unless you deal with his anti-Christian presuppositions, all the evidence in the world will not convince him of the bodily resurrection of Jesus Christ. He assumes the following things.

      1. The universe is a self-contained, closed system.
      2. Everything happens according to natural law and can be explained by natural law.
      3. No miracles or supernatural intervention are possible. Therefore, he concludes, the resurrection of anyone including Christ is impossible.

   B. *Are there common presuppositions which are generally shared by most non-Christian systems?* Yes!
      1. *Human Autonomy:* The assumption that man starting from himself by himself without any outside special revelation can arrive at a true understanding of himself and the world around him with all the inter-relationships involved.
      2. *Ontological Thinking:* The assumption that whatever is "thinkable" to you exists and whatever is "unthinkable" cannot exist. Reality corresponds to what you think it to be.
      3. *Monism:* The assumption that ultimate reality is of one kind or essence of being, i.e., there is no qualitative difference between objects. Things differ only quantitatively in terms of a different

arrangement of general being. Reality is viewed in terms of a scale of being.

VII. Questions concerning the *individual concepts* of the non-Christian system.

A. *Are there any concepts here which are borrowed from the Christian system?* Yes.

B. *Are these concepts consistent with non-Christian presuppositions?* No.
Example: You meet a non-Christian who believes in civil rights and in the dignity and oneness of mankind. You challenge his right to believe in such things because he has certain presuppositions which contradict these ideas. He assumes that the theory of evolution is true and that man is an animal who has fought his way to the top by the survival of the fittest. He rejects the biblical account of Adam and Eve. You press him until he admits that on the basis of his evolutionary presuppositions, the different races are probably different species of animals which evolved from different ancestral origins. Once he admits this, he must recognize that he cannot believe in the equality, dignity and oneness of mankind and believe in evolution at the same time.

C. *Are these concepts consistent with each other?* No.
Example: Sartre and the Algerian Manifesto (1960) are good illustrations of conflicting concepts. On the one hand, he believed that, since God did not exist, there was no infinite point of reference from which meaning could be given to particulars. Thus there are no absolute moral laws. On the other hand, Sartre signed the Algerian Manifesto which was a protest statement against the Algerian War.[5] It is obvious that you cannot say that God does not exist and that any war is wrong at the same time. Without God there is no day of judgment, no ultimate justice, and no ultimate standard for right or wrong. We do not have any sufficient basis to say that anyone is wrong or right and reject God at the same time.

D. *Are these concepts coherent? Are they understandable as a whole and in their parts?* No.
Example: When the pre-Socratic Greek philosopher Crytalus was asked what he believed, all he would do was wiggle his little finger. He would not speak a single word. Thus whatever he believed, it certainly was not comprehensible.

---

5. Francis A. Schaeffer, *How Should We Then Live?*, Fleming H. Revell Company, Old Tappan, N.J., pp. 167-68.

One friend was disturbed because, while he was high on certain drugs, he thought he was writing tremendous philosophical essays and composing brilliant pieces of music but when finally down and sober he always discovered complete confusion and incoherence. Reality demands coherence while fantasy can play around with the absurd.

E. *Are these concepts cohesive? Do these concepts hang together?* No.
Example: A box of unconnected pearls do not manifest any order or meaning. But if we put them on a string, then they can become something meaningful like a necklace or a bracelet. In the same way, many people do not try to correlate their ideas. They simply pick up an idea here and there without any attempt to relate them to each other or to bring any cohesiveness to these ideas.

F. *Are these concepts self-refuting? Do they carry within themselves the seeds of their own destruction?* Yes.
Example: Hegel destroyed himself by his concept of the dialectic process of truth. If truth is not found at any point of the thesis-antithesis-synthesis process but is only found at the ultimate end of the process, then Hegel's own philosophy is not true because it is only a part of the dialectic process. If Hegel is right—he is wrong!

G. *Can these concepts stand up to a rigorous exposure to the Law of Contradiction?* No.
Example: Hegel logically established the Law of Contradiction when he denied it, for to deny anything you must use the Law of Contradiction.

H. *Can those who hold to these concepts believe what they live and live what they believe?* No.
Example: The famous modern musician John Cage believes that chance underlies reality. Therefore music should reflect this contingency. Yet, he picks mushrooms as a hobby. It is obvious that he would not live very long if he picked and ate mushrooms on the basis of chance. He cannot live what he believes.[6]

I. *Are these concepts verifiable? Do they correspond with what is there? Can we investigate the claims of these concepts?* No.
Example: Behaviorists claim that "man is a mechanized animal and everything he does is predetermined by chemical and environmental factors." This concept of determinism is set forth by many modern scientists. Yet, this theory does not correspond with the evidence.[7]

---

6. Ibid., pp. 194-95.
7. Francis A. Schaeffer, *Back to Freedom and Dignity,* Inter-Varsity Press, Downers Grove, Ill., 1973.

1. We can point to art since machines and animals do not produce art.
2. Others point to the lack of factual evidence for determinism.
3. Others point to psychological evidence which proves that man is not a machine and that man is ultimately free.

VIII. Questions concerning the *logical outcome* of the system.

A. *Where will this system ultimately take us if we allow it to be consistent? Where will we end up if we follow it to its logical conclusion?*

In the Christian view of reality there exists God, angelic beings, man, animals, plants, and things. In the non-Christian system, once the biblical God is rejected there begins a destructive process which ultimately brings man down to the level of an impersonal object such as a rock or stone. For example, once we say, "God is dead," there is no reason to believe in angels, no reason to see man as unique and apart from the animals, no reason to separate animal life from plant life, and no reason not to look at all things including man merely as material objects which are either "useful" or "in the way" of the upward evolutionary process.

The destruction of hope, love, morals, meaning and significance is complete once man is reduced to the level of a machine. The theories and actions of the godless communists must be understood in this light. When they murder millions of people who are in their estimation "unproductive" and "reactionary," they are just being consistent.

PART THREE

THE CHRISTIAN WORLD AND LIFE VIEW

I. Introductory Remarks
   A. Our goal: To review briefly the Christian system.
   B. Importance: It is not only necessary to defend the faith (Jude 3) but we must intelligently explain it to others (I Peter 3:15).

II. Discussion from Diagram #2
   A. *The Person*
     1. Spiritual regeneration has taken place and now the person both sees and enters the kingdom of God (John 3:1-16).
     2. The mind has been opened to understand Christianity in a unique way known only to believers (Luke 24:45).
     3. The heart has been predisposed by the Spirit to receive the Christian message (Acts 16:14).
   B. *The Faith*
     1. The Christian faith is not a humanistic leap in the dark. It is not a leap into non-reason.
     2. Faith is given by the Holy Spirit (Phil. 1:29; Eph. 2:8).
     3. Faith is guided by the Holy Spirit (John 16:13).
     4. Faith rests on the objective Word of God, the Holy Scriptures.
   C. *The Presuppositions*
     1. They are revealed in the Holy Scriptures and are found nowhere else.
     2. According to the Bible, Creation-Fall-Redemption are the foundational presuppositions which make up the biblical world and life view. To understand anything correctly is to view it in the light of these basic truths of the Bible.
       a. These truths are put first in the Bible because they are *foundational* to all that follow. Genesis 1-3 simply unfolds the three truths of Creation-Fall-Redemption.

b. *Thematically,* everything else in Scripture is a development of these three themes. In the Old Testament and in the New Testament we are constantly reminded of these three great events.

c. *Exegetically,* these three truths serve as spectacles or glasses through which we can understand and deal with present problems and issues.

When Jesus dealt with the issue of marriage and divorce, He approached it in terms of what marriage originally was at the creation and thus "ought" to be. Then He looked at the issue from the perspective of the fall, for sin explains why divorce was granted to man (See Matt. 19:1-6).

The apostle Paul used Creation-Fall-Redemption as the spectacles through which he could examine from the biblical perspective: (1) the respective roles and functions of male and female in the context of the home and in the church (I Cor. 11:3-12; I Tim. 2:12-14); (2) whether certain foods are "evil" and should not be eaten by Christians (I Tim. 4:1-5); (3) why the creation is in a state of "groaning and travailing" and why the Christian has hope that the creation shall be delivered from the evil effects of Adam's fall into sin (Rom. 8:18-23).

D. *The Concepts*

1. Starting with the given presuppositions of Holy Scripture, we can develop the Christian position on many things in direct opposition to the opposing non-Christian concepts. In the following examples the Christian position is stated and then the opposing non-Christian concept is given.

   a. From the presupposition of *creation.*

   (1) The world was created out of nothing versus the eternity of matter or energy.

   (2) The Creator-creature distinction versus all forms of monism.

   (3) The reality of matter versus all forms of spiritualism.

   (4) The reality of spirit versus all forms of materialism.

   (5) The goodness of matter versus the evil of matter.

   (6) The fact of divine order and plan behind the creation versus the concept of ultimate chance or contingency.

   (7) Beginning with the personal versus beginning with the impersonal.

   (8) Man as a unique creature created in God's image with singular dignity and importance versus man as an animal kicked up by some fluke of chance in the blind and meaningless

evolutionary process.

    (9) The oneness of humanity versus racism.

  b. From the presupposition of the *fall.*

    Definition of original sin: Man's attempt to be autonomous and independent of God. Genesis 3 reveals that man was tempted on three levels: (a) metaphysical: Satan said, *"Be* what you want to be,'' (b) epistemological: Satan argued, *"Know* what you want to know,'' (c) ethical: Satan demanded, *"Do* what you want to do.''

    (1) The creation is now sub-normal versus the world is normal.

    (2) Man is now sub-normal versus man is normal.

    (3) Man's problems are rooted in the ethical and not in the metaphysical versus man's problem is his humanity and his finiteness.

  c. From the presupposition of *redemption.*

    (1) Salvation is something initiated, planned, and accomplished by the triune God of Father, Son and Holy Spirit versus all forms of self-saving religions.

    (2) Biblical salvation concerns individuals and sees to it that they remain and retain their own unique personality versus impersonalism and nihilism.

    (3) Salvation is cosmic in scope versus soul saving only (Rom. 8:21; II Peter 3; Rev. 21).

2. The biblical world and life view meets all the tests of a valid system. The Christian concepts are:

  a. Consistent with each other as well as being consistent with their presuppositions.

  b. Coherent and cohesive.

  c. Not self-refuting and self-destructive.

  d. In full accord with the Law of Contradiction because the Law of Contradiction itself is based upon the biblical view of God's ontological nature. Since God cannot lie (Titus 1:2), the Law of Contradiction is an aspect of God's very being.

  e. Verifiable and does, in fact, correspond with what is there.
Example: A survey of biblical archeology will reveal irrefutable verification of the biblical system through fulfilled prophecy.[8]

  f. Livable. The Christian is the only one who can live what he believes and believe what he lives. Everything in his life

---

8. See J. A. Thompson, *The Bible and Archaeology,* Wm. B. Eerdmans Publishing Company, Grand Rapids, Mich., 1962.

17

corresponds exactly to the biblical world and life view.
E. *The logical conclusion of the Christian system*
　1. Ultimate meaning and significance for all things including man versus existentialism's meaninglessness.
　2. Absolute ethical standards versus all forms of relativism and situational ethics.
　3. Brings hope, love and life to light through the gospel of Jesus Christ versus ultimate despair.

PART FOUR

APPLICATIONS OF THE
CHRISTIAN WORLD AND LIFE VIEW

The following applications are not intended to be exhaustive studies of any of the topics examined. The following examples are suggested outlines which illustrate how to apply the Christian perspective of creation, fall, and redemption to all of life. It is hoped that these illustrations will motivate others to do exhaustive treatments of important topics from the Christian perspective.

I. A Christian View of Ethics
    A. In view of the creation of both the world and man
        1. Christian ethics is based upon the Creator-creature relationship.
            a. Man was created dependent upon God his Creator for all things.
            b. Man was not created autonomous, i.e., independent of God and dependent only upon himself. He was not created to be a truth-maker or an ethic-maker. He was made to think God's thoughts after Him, i.e., to be a truth-receiver. He was made to be an ethic-receiver, i.e., to reflect ethically God's moral character as God's image-bearer.
            c. All apostate ethical theories assume that man is autonomous. They assume that man can create or discover his own ethics by starting with himself and from himself and that man does not need any outside special word revelation.
        2. The importance of pre-fall special Word revelation
            a. Since man was created dependent upon his Creator, it is not surprising to find that Genesis 1-3 reveals that *God spoke to man in words which man could understand.* God told Adam what man's task in life was and ethically what was his duty and what was forbidden. *From the very beginning of creation, man was dependent upon special word revelation for his ethics.*
            God spoke to man because God never intended man to make or discover his ethics solely from:

19

(1) general revelation
(2) the image of God
(3) his moral image
(4) his reason or logic
(5) instinct or intuition
(6) insight into the situation which would reveal supposed "laws" of nature or creation "norms."

   b. Apostate ethical theories either deny or ignore pre-fall special Word revelation because they want man to be free from any supernaturally revealed absolute ethical standards. They base their ethics on the assumption that man can discover or create his own ethics apart from special revelation by looking to one, some or all of the six sources listed above. Even alleged "Christian" ethical theories will often picture man at creation as knowing instinctively, intuitionally, or by insight into general revelation what his task in life was, and that he was not to eat of the tree of the knowledge of good and evil and that to eat of the other trees was ethically good. They attempt to free man from revealed ethical standards in order to establish human autonomy.[9]

B. In view of the fall of man into sin and guilt
  1. The fall supplies us with the only valid explanation of the present ethical confusion and tension. The existence of sin, evil, death, war, pain, etc. can be and must be understood in terms of the historical fall of Adam and Eve into sin.
  2. The biblical doctrine of total depravity reveals that:
    a. Man is alienated from God's revealed ethical standards because he hates God and His law and will not submit to it and, indeed, he no longer has the spiritual ability to obey the law from the heart (Rom. 8:7-8).
    b. Man is now predisposed to choose the wrong, believe the false, and feel the evil and wicked (John 3:19-20).
    c. Man will seek to escape God's revealed ethics by:
      (1) rejecting the idea of revealed absolutes;
      (2) saying that God's law was only for the people to whom He revealed the law and that it has no bearing today on our ethics;
      (3) pretending that we can discover God's ethics by looking into

9. See the author's *The Dooyeweerdian Concept of the Word of God,* (Presbyterian & Reformed Publishing Co.), for an exposure of one such "Christian" situational ethics position.

the creation or the situation using the light of love and reason to reveal man's ethics. Some have pretended that God did not actually reveal the law to Moses by *talking* to Moses and by actually *writing* the law on the tablets with His own finger. But, rather, they say that Moses got the law by "insight" into the creation and into the situation in which he found himself. Thus we can discover ethics for today by "insight."

3. The fall did not do away with God's revealed ethics for man. But, instead, it made necessary more and greater special revelation which would show man in detail how and in what ways he is to be an image-bearer of God. The moral law of God is simply God's revelation of the ethical aspects of His own being which man is to reflect. *Example:* Since God does not lie, man is told not to lie (Titus 1:2; Exod. 20:16).

4. Apostate theories of ethics usually assume the following things.
Major premise: What is, is normal.
Minor premise: What is normal, is right.
Conclusion: What is, is right.
The biblical truth of the fall reveals the fallacy of the major premise; for what is, is not normal, since what is, is not what once was; and neither is it what it shall be. What is, is not "right," for it is not what "ought" to be. "Oughtness" belongs to what man was at creation when he was perfect in righteousness, holiness, and knowledge. The "ought" and "right" of creation is the standard which judges and condemns what is now.

5. If man in the original creation needed special word revelation to give him his ethics, how much more does fallen man need and depend upon God's special Word revelation—the Holy Scriptures! In the Bible we find moral absolutes which are binding on man the image-bearer at all times.

6. Apostate ethical theories which claim to be "Christian" will often state that special revelation was given only because and after man fell into sin. They tell us that man does not need special Word revelation as *man* but as *sinner.* But this is manifestly false because man as man was the recipient of special Word revelation from the very moment of creation. *The fall into sin did not bring special revelation into being. Rather, it was the rejection of special revelation that brought the fall into being* (Gen. 3:1-6). Satan's plan to tempt man to sin against God began by casting doubt on the absolute and universally binding character of God's revealed ethic for man. "Hath God said?" (Gen. 3:1).

21

7. The fall makes necessary a full disclosure of man's sin. God's revealed law ethic for man has as one of its functions the driving of sinners to Christ for forgiveness. The law exists to show us that we are sinners in order to bring us to Christ (Rom. 3:20; 7:7; Gal. 3:24).

C. In view of redemption

   1. Christ Jesus came and perfectly obeyed God's revealed law ethic for man in order to fulfill all righteousness (Matt. 3:15; 5:17; Gal. 4:4,5). His obedience to the law is the basis of justification. Through union with Christ we are declared ethically perfect and without guilt (Rom. 5:1).

   2. The Holy Spirit comes into the heart of the believer and causes him to love the law and to obey it from the heart. Love for God does not negate the law or substitute for it. Jesus said, "If you love me *you will keep my commandments*" (John 14:15; cf. I John 2:3,4).

   3. Redemption does not do away with special word revelation but, instead, it makes greater and more detailed special word revelation necessary, for the gospel cannot be found in general revelation. True saving faith can come only through hearing the written Word of God, the biblical gospel (Rom. 10:17).

   4. Apostate ethical theories which claim to be "Christian" will sometimes teach that redemption does away with revealed ethics and man is now to derive his ethics from his "insight" into the "laws" or "norms" in the given situation. The law of God is now supposedly supplanted by love. But this is manifestly false for redemption was not accomplished to make conformity to God's ethical or moral character no longer necessary as if man's purpose is no longer to bear God's image. Rather, redemption comes so that we may be recreated in God's image and conformed to the moral law which reveals how man may ethically reflect God's character in this world. Man was once perfectly conformed to God's ethic. The fall made man a sinner who hates God's ethic and who seeks to set up his own ethical standards. Redemption comes to enable man to once again render perfect obedience to the law of God out of love (Rom. 8:4).

Note on Situation Ethics

1. While the fallacy of situation eithics can be demonstrated by pointing out the anti-biblical presuppositions which underlie it and the invalid method of

22

arguing from highly irrelevant stories and situations, the death blow to all forms of so-called "Christian" situation ethics is found in I Corinthians 10:13 which says that because God is faithful we will *never* find ourselves in a situation where we *must* sin but there will *always* be a way to escape. We never have to sin to make grace abound (Rom. 6:1). God never puts us in a situation or calls upon us to break one of His revealed ethical laws in order to keep another one of His laws. A Christian must never say or feel that he "must" or "ought" to break God's laws. The Bible does not teach that anyone in any situation "ought" to sin.

2. The situation ethics people will respond by trying to picture a situation in which they feel that they "must" sin because it is what they "ought" to do. Once the sin is viewed as a "must" and as an "ought," it is justified and magically transformed into being "good."

3. A Christian view of ethics will reject each of the constructed situations which the situational ethicist puts out because the situation described does not take into account several things.

   a. God's sovereignty is not taken into account. Since no one knows the future and what God may do even in terms of extraordinary providence, no one can say that "unless you sin these people will die." God will always make a way for the people of God to escape sinning. His sovereignty guarantees it. God is still alive today.

   b. The power of the Holy Spirit is never taken into account. The believer does not have to worry about what he would say if he found himself in any of the weird and highly unlikely situations which are put forward by situation ethics proponents because he has the promise of Jesus, "do not be anxious about how or what you will speak; for it shall be given you in that hour what you are to speak. For it is not you who speaks, but it is the Spirit of your Father who speaks in you" (Matt. 10:19-20). We are to "trust the Lord with all our hearts and lean not to our own understanding." As we do this in the area of ethics, as in all of life, we will find that "He will direct" our path (Prov. 3:5,6).

   c. Even though God is faithful in making a way for us to escape sinning, the believer to his shame is not always faithful in using the escape and thus he sins. The believer is then directed by Scripture to seek forgiveness through the cleansing blood of Jesus (I John 1:7–2:2). But situation ethics never points you to the blood of Jesus Christ. Instead of leading men to the cross, situation ethics rationalizes the sin away. They seek to hide their sins by pretending that they "had" to sin or they did what was "necessary" and what "ought" to be done. Since the sin was "necessary," they are not really responsible! Thus God will not judge them for it. So why confess it? There

23

is no place in situation ethics for the necessary blood atonement of Christ, the need to come before God for forgiveness or the pain of repentance and confession. Situation ethics is but one sad and tragic attempt of rebellious sinners to overthrow God's revealed ethic and to escape the judgment on the Last Day.[10]

d. Situation ethics is actually blasphemy because it pictures God as being either ignorant or stupid. God is ignorant in that He did not foresee that His laws would contradict each other at times and that His people would have to break one law in order to keep another. Or, God is stupid because He foresaw that His laws would contradict each other and that they would force His people to sin that grace may abound but He could not figure out any way to deal with the problem.

II. A Christian View of Art
  A. In view of creation
    1. The biblical account of creation supplies us with the only valid basis for a proper understanding of the origin, existence, function, and explanation of art.
      a. Art is not a fluke of the evolutionary process. It is part of the image of God in which man was created.
      b. Man's aesthetic being is patterned after God's aesthetic being. Animals and machines do not produce or appreciate art. But man as God's image-bearer is both an art-maker and an art-appreciator. Art is part of human existence from the very beginning because it is based on the Creator-creature relationship.
      c. Man as image-bearer was given the cultural mandate in Genesis 1:28-30. Man's art was intended to be a vital part of his obedience to this mandate.
      d. After the work of creation was finished, God looked over all He had made and "behold, it was very good," i.e., the creation was *beautiful* as well as perfect.

      The goodness of the creation means that no art medium is intrinsically evil. We must never say that any particular combination of sounds, forms, colors, or textures is intrinsically evil. Too many Christians have fallen into a Platonic view of reality in which matter is viewed as being evil. Thus some fundamentalists have taught that certain types of music and certain art forms of modern

---

10. See: John Murray, *Principles of Christian Conduct,* Wm. B. Eerdmans Pub. Co., Grand Rapids, Mich., 1957, pp. 123-148.

art are intrinsically un-Christian, evil and Satanic.

 e. Christian art should, at times, reflect the original creation in all of its beauty, form, harmony and goodness. *Example:* David wrote psalms which celebrate creation by using the medium of poetry, song and instrumental music (Ps. 8; 19; 89; 100, etc.). Franz Joseph Haydn's *Creation* is another good example of an artistic display of the beauty of the original creation.

 f. Creation alone supplies us with a valid basis upon which to explain the origin, existence, function and diversification of color. The theory of evolution can never explain why a black cow will eat green grass and produce white milk. The Christian knows that color is here in all of its diversification simply because God likes color.

2. Beauty is ultimately in the eye of *the Beholder*—God the Creator. God Himself is the original artist who is the aesthetic pattern for man who was created in God's image. There is an aesthetic aspect to God's being and work.

 a. When we look at the world of color and form which God created (such as a beautiful sunset), we must confess that God is the great Painter.

 b. When we examine the shape of the mountains, the different forms of animal and plant life, and the human body, we know that God is the great Sculptor.

 c. When we read in the Scripture that God surrounds Himself with angelic choirs and the songs of redeemed sinners, that the angelic choirs sang their heavenly music at the birth of Christ, that the stars sing for joy, that God made musical instruments in heaven to be played continuously before Him, and that God has commanded men to worship Him through music, we know that He is the great Musician (Rev. 5:8; 14:1-3; Luke 2:13, 14; Job 38:7; Ps. 30:4; 33:3).

 d. When we examine the literary forms within Scripture, we find beautiful poetry, prayer, prose, praise and proclamation. Thus we must confess that God is the great Poet and Writer.

3. Art is not for art's sake. Art ultimately exists for God's glory for He is here and is not silent. Thus the bird singing in the forest where no human ear can hear is still beautiful because God hears it. The dessert flower which no human eye has ever seen is still beautiful because God sees it.

B. In view of the fall
   1. The biblical account of the fall supplies us with the only valid way to understand the origin and existence of ugliness, evil, pain, suffering, chaos, war, death, sorrow, etc. What is now is not what originally was.
   2. The aesthetic aspect of the image of God in man was corrupted by man's fall into sin, for the fall polluted every aspect of man's being. Man's aesthetic abilities are now used against God instead of for God. Thus we find the rise of apostate art which finds its climax in idolatry where the art object is worshiped as God. Idolatry reveals that man now worships the creature instead of the Creator (Rom. 1:18-25).
   3. Christian art should, at times, reflect the ugliness and the death of man which sin causes. It should reveal the misery, agony, and pain of hell. It should point to the ultimate despair of a life without God. Christian art should portray the horror of hopeless sinners in the past who were the recipients of the great judgments of God against sin. *Example:* the flood.
   4. Christian art should supply the mediums through which the people of God can express their own despair, conviction of sin, confusion, pain, discouragement, etc. We need "songs in the night," songs when loved ones die, songs of confession of sin. The psalms give us many examples of this kind of art (Ps. 51, etc.)
   5. The Christian artist should aesthetically surpass the pessimistic existentialist artist when it comes to portraying the despair, ugliness and hopelessness of man. The doctrine of total depravity as taught in such places as Ephesians 2:1-3, 12 is more realistic and frightening than anything the humanists can come up with. We need aesthetically to confront man with the ugliness and horror of his rebellion against God and with the reality of divine judgment against sin.
C. In view of redemption
   1. We are to reclaim every square inch of this world for Christ. Every thought and talent is to be redeemed unto God's glory for all of life is to be lived for Him (I Cor. 10:31; II Cor. 10:5). All of culture is to be conquered for Christ. Even though sin makes it impossible to attain total perfection in this life, Christians are given the Spirit of God to execute this mandate as much as possible in all of culture. When Jesus returns and creates a new earth, then the redeemed will fulfill the original mandate given to Adam. Our wildest dreams cannot comprehend the wondrous art which shall be produced by the glorified saints in the eternal state.

2. Redemption supplies us with the only valid basis for Christians going into the arts, for it is through Christ alone that we can escape from apostate art. Redeemed sinners respond aesthetically to God because the image of God is renewed within them (Eph. 4:24; 5:18, 19). The arts should be viewed as:
   a. The saints at worship, praise, rest, recreation, prayer, confession of sin, etc. (Ps. 19; 23; 51; 90; 100).
   b. The saints' obedience to the culture mandate (Gen. 1:28).
   c. The saints' stewardship of God-given talents (Matt. 25:14-30).
   d. The saints' obedience to the mission mandate (Matt. 28:19, 20).
3. Christian art should at times reflect the great moments in the history of redemption, the thanks, prayer, and praise of redeemed sinners, and the saints' desire for the lost to be saved. Again, many of David's psalms are artistic expressions of thankfulness to God for salvation (Ps. 103, etc.).
4. From the standpoint of redemption, Christian art should at times reveal the following:
   a. God is there and is not silent.
   b. There is hope, love, meaning, truth, etc.
   c. The beauty and dignity of Christ.
   d. There is order behind the chaos of life. God is still in control.
   e. The beauty that will be in the new creation.
   f. That the good will ultimately triumph over the evil.
   g. That the righteous will be vindicated.
5. Christian artists engaged in evangelism should attempt to push sinners to despair in order to drive them to Christ. We should reveal both the ugliness of sin and the beauty of salvation. In this sense every artist is an evangelist to a lost, sick and dying world, for every Christian is scripturally called to evangelize his world for Christ.
6. The Christian artist should be viewed as a prophet, priest and king to the people of God.
   a. As a prophet, he should convey the truth through his art.
   b. As a priest, he should lead God's people in their worship of God through the arts.
   c. As a king, he should provide for the aesthetic needs of the people of God and protect them from apostate art which leads to idolatry.
7. Perhaps it would be helpful to see that art has various functions. The following describes some of these functions. A given piece of art may have one, some, or all of these functions:
   a. "Cool" art: art aimed at creating a distinct mood, impression or

emotion on those exposed to the art. *Example:* Psalm 150.

    b. "Hot" art: art aimed at communicating truth to the intellect. This can be called "message art." *Example:* Psalm 1 and Proverbs.

    c. Reflective art: art which expresses and reflects the mood and emotional state of the artist. *Example:* Psalm 51.

    d. Aesthetic art: art aimed purely at the aesthetic sense of man. It is "beautiful" without being cool, hot or reflective. It is for entertainment purposes. This is art for beauty's sake. *Example:* the art work in the tabernacle and temple (Exod. 25; II Chron. 3:6).

    e. Enrichment art, i.e., the "hidden art" of daily life: flower arrangements, table settings, attention to the selection of color of different foods, etc. This is art in which every home should be involved.

D. Closing thoughts

    1. *Is it proper to distinguish between secular and religious art?* Answer: Yes/No. Yes, if you mean the distinction between art which portrays a biblical or "religious" event or scene and art which has a non-biblical subject as its focus. There is a difference between a picture showing the flood and one showing a country picnic.

       No, if you mean that only religious art is "Christian art." Christian art is not restricted to events of biblical history, for the entire world is God's world (Ps. 24).

       Also, all art is "religious" in the sense of being either apostate or God-glorifying. There is not any "secular" art in the sense of "neutral" art.

    2. *Can a Christian artist do art to entertain people?* Answer: We are to glorify God and to *enjoy* Him forever. Entertainment and recreation are legitimate creature necessities and are, therefore, legitimate fields of work for the Christian. Those who are negative and suspicious of entertainment reveal a hidden strain of Platonic thinking.

    3. *Should we judge a work of art on the basis of the life style of the artist?* Answer: No, just as we can take a crooked stick and draw a straight line, even so wicked men can produce good art through common grace.

    4. *Can a Christian artist do "cool," reflective, or aesthetic art or must he restrict himself to portraying and conveying the gospel through "hot" art?* Answer: The Christian is not restricted to any one particular function or form of art. A still life painting of a bowl of fruit is just as "Christian" as a painting of the crucifixion if it is done for God's glory. The artist is not restricted to "hot" art.

5. *Is "good" art determined on the basis of the intent of the artist or on the amount of biblical truth it conveys?* Answer: The quality of a work of art is not determined solely on the basis of the intent of the artist or the clarity of its message. A Christian artist can produce poor art even though he did it for God's glory and tried to convey the gospel. The quality of art is determined by such aspects as Dr. Schaeffer has outlined in *Art and the Bible* or on what Dr. Kuyper has stated in his chapter on "Calvinism and Art" in *Lectures on Calvinism*. Schaeffer mentions the following criteria:
   a. Technical excellence
   b. Validity
   c. Intellectual content, the world view which comes through the art
   d. The integration of content and vehicle

III. A Christian View of History

We must begin by making the distinction between history and the study of history. History is the unfolding of God's plan; the study of history is man's attempt to record and interpret what has happened in the past.[11]

A. History
   1. *In View of Creation*
      a. History has a beginning and an end versus cyclical views of history.
      b. History is the unfolding of God's plan versus history as an aimless and meaningless evolutionary process.
      c. History has ultimate meaning and significance since all history will glorify God versus history viewed in terms of meaninglessness, operationalism, utilitarianism, pragmatism, etc.
   2. *In View of the Fall*
      a. History reflects the chaos and crime of man's sin.
      b. History reflects the existence of evil (war, death, floods, etc.).
      c. History reflects the judgment of God upon man for his sin (the flood, Canaan, etc.).
   3. *In View of Redemption*
      a. God acts in history as a true agent versus the popular modern supra-history theories. *Example:* Karl Barth's salvation history theory.
      b. History is moving to a redemptive climax, for the world which now exists will be destroyed, and a new earth will be created versus the theory that the earth will continue as it always has.

---

11. See: Rousas J. Rushdoony, *The Biblical Philosophy of History*, Presbyterian & Reformed Pub. Co., Nutley, N.J., 1969.

c. God orders history for the good of the elect (Rom. 8:28).
B. The Study of History
1. Man as God's image-bearer can have a finite but true knowledge of history versus history as unknowable.
2. The study of history is one of the sciences which covers all other sciences (history of math, history of society, history of economics, etc.).
3. No science is objective or neutral. Therefore the study of history is guided by one's presuppositions.
4. The study of history primarily concerns man as a culture-former in his reactions to God, his fellow man and the world around him. It includes God's intervention into human affairs.
5. We must avoid all reductionistic historical methods. *Example:*
   a. Hegel reshaped history to conform to his thesis-antithesis-synthesis model.
   b. Communistic economic reductionism reshapes history into class struggles.
   c. Fall of Rome. What caused it? Typical reductionistic reasoning will ascribe Rome's fall to only one of the following causes:
      (1) Political—pagans caused it.
      (2) Economic—inflation caused it.
      (3) Cultural—slavery caused it.
      (4) Religious—Christianity caused it.
      The Christian approach avoids the reductionistic thinking by stating that:
         (a) Ultimately, Rome fell simply because God willed it (Dan. 4). God's sovereignty should be stressed.
         (b) There were many things which God used to accomplish His plan. Thus some of the reasons given above are valid.
6. Moral judgments concerning people and their actions are possible only upon a Christian basis. *Example:*
   a. Hitler was evil.
   b. Greed drove the Spanish to explore South America for gold while religious persecution drove the Pilgrims to North America for God.
7. We must reject the pretended historical neutrality and objectivity of humanistic historians even though the myth of objectivity has a stranglehold on most modern historians. Christian historians must be radical enough to escape the influence of this myth. God did and still

does act in history. God did raise up Luther and Calvin. When humanists and misguided Christian historians accuse great Christian historians such as D'Aubigne of writing "biased" and "purple-prose" history, they reveal that they themselves are actually the real myth-makers who are pretending that God did not act in history. D'Aubigne represents the highest standards for Christian historians who have not been duped by the myth that scholarship means neutrality.

IV. A Christian View of Psychology

   A. Your *anthropology*, i.e., your view of man's nature, origin and relationship to the rest of the creation, will determine your view of the nature, function and methods of human psychology.

     Example 1. Typical non-Christian anthropologies view man as being an animal produced by the evolutionary process. Thus some non-Christian psychological theories seek to explain human behavior in terms of comparative animal behavior and evolution. The behavior of primates, mice, etc., is assumed to be the key in the explanation and interpretation of human behavior.

     Example 2. Christian anthropology views man as being a unique creature created in God's image. As such, he relates to the divine as well as to the earthly.

     In that man is created in God's image, he has an immortal personal soul, but in that he is finite and has a body, man will be similar in some bodily functions to animals (which do not have personal souls).

     Although there are comparative bodily and mental functions between man and animals due to both having finite bodies, human psychology cannot be explained simply by the observation of the actions of animals. A man is not a monkey or a mouse and it is foolish to think that man can be explained simply by observing animals in laboratory experiments or in the wild.

   B. Human psychology must take into account the fourfold state of man.

     1. *In View of Creation:* Adam and Eve did not have any psychological problems within themselves or any problems relating to God, other people, or the world around them.

     2. *In View of the Fall:* Because of (a) moral alienation from God through hatred in his heart toward God, (b) inward conflict due to lust, pride, envy, etc., and (c) problems relating to other sinners and the hostile world around him, man is beset by many psychological ills. All psychological problems are rooted either in sin or in the effects of sin. Thus the basis of man's problems is moral and not

31

his humanity. Even chemical, glandular, or physical problems are rooted in the effects of the fall because all pain, sickness, and death came to be through sin.

3. *In View of Redemption:* When salvation takes place, man's moral alienation from God is removed and the love and peace of God is shed abroad in the heart by the Holy Spirit who comes to dwell with the believer and his problems. After all, does the unbeliever have the indwelling Spirit? Is his conscience renewed? Is he convicted of sin by God? Does the blood of Jesus wash away the guilt and defilement of his sin? It is a shame that even supposedly Christian psychologists lump Christians and non-Christians together in their theories and therapy. (The English Puritans had great insights into the psychology of the believer.)

4. *Man after Death:*
   a. The saints in heaven: once again there are no psychological problems. The process of being conformed to Christ which was begun in regeneration and carried on in sanctification is now completed in heaven. There needs to be a psychology of the blessed.
   b. The wicked in hell: the weeping, wailing, cursing, gnashing of teeth, etc., which Jesus and the apostles used to describe the agonies of hell should lead to a psychology of hell.

C. The Scriptures supply us with a good amount of material on many psychological topics.

Example 1. A psychology of atheism and unbelief can be developed from Romans 1, 2, 8 and I Corinthians 1-4, etc. The Christian should explore the psycho-spiritual causes behind the unregenerate's rejection of the gospel. Bill Gothard's "Basic Youth Conflict" series has some excellent material. See also *The Psychology of Atheism* by R. C. Sproul.

Example 2. A psychology of conscience formation and function can be developed from the Scriptures. Professor Dr. J. O'Donnell at Nyack College has done some good work on this topic.

V. A Christian View of Marriage

A. Marriage in view of creation

The biblical account and concept of creation supplies us with the only valid way of understanding the origin, purpose and significance of marriage.

1. The origin of marriage: According to the biblical account and concept of creation, marriage is not a social contract or institution which developed in human culture through a blind and meaningless evolutionary process. Marriage is the creation of God and is, therefore, a

divine institution.

As a divine institution, marriage and the family belong to God. Thus God has a right to set up or structure marriage and the family any way He pleases. The original marriage of Adam and Eve constitutes the standard for all future marriages. We can now state that what marriage "ought" to be should be patterned after what it originally was in the Garden of Eden. The first marriage is the prototype for all future marriages.

2. The purpose of marriage: Marriage was instituted by God as being the best way of ordering human relationships which would give God the most glory and man the most good. Marriage is for God's glory.

Marriage should reflect the beauty and harmony which is in the triune Godhead. As the heavenly family of Father, Son, and Holy Spirit work together in wondrous harmony born out of their infinite love for each other, even so the human family should reflect the love, harmony, and intimate communication within the Trinity.

It is also obvious that marriage was instituted by God to be the stable context within which human sexuality could be fulfilled in the procreation of children. When God created Eve and gave her to Adam, we must realize that this marriage was the only way to fulfill the cultural mandate to fill the earth with mankind. Adam and Eve were the first husband and wife and then, as God intended, the first parents.

Marriage was instituted in order to make man complete, for God said, "It is not good that the man should be alone; I will make him an help meet for him" (Gen. 2:18).

Adam needed a companion who would share all of life with him. Thus we must say that God never intended for anyone to be alone and lonely. For every person there should be a companion for life.

If the world would have continued in sinless perfection, there would never have been any lonely or unloved people. Every person would know the joy of loving and being loved as God intended.

It is only upon the basis of Christian theology that marriage and the family can be viewed as having dignity, validity and true significance. As Hebrews 13:4 states, "Marriage is honourable; let us keep it so, and the marriage-bond inviolate; for God's judgment will fall on fornicators and adulterers" (NEB).

3. The significance of marriage: The first marriage took place when Adam and Eve reached maturity in every area of their lives. When they reached sexual maturity and puberty, they were also ready for all the responsibilities of married life. Thus neither of them

experienced sexual frustration or desired sexual deviation.

Since marriage and family belong to God, we must follow the structure of marriage which God instituted in the Garden. Adam was the head of the family and Eve was submissive to his headship. This structure is what "ought" to be in every marriage. Thus the Women's Liberation Movement is in open violation of God's creation ordinance of marriage when it denies the man's headship over the woman.

While the male and female are equal in terms of their *being* or *nature*, seeing that they are both (1) equally created in God's image, (2) equally sinners before God and, (3) recipients of the same benefits of salvation, nevertheless, the Scriptures also teach that they are not equal in terms of *function* or *office*. Man's headship did not arise because of the fall or as a result of Hebrew culture. Man was the head of the woman at creation as a direct institution of God Himself (I Cor. 11:3, 7-9; I Tim. 2:12, 13).

The first marriage as it came from God's hand was perfect in every respect. There were no problems in the marriage. Therefore we must look to the fall as the origin of marital problems.

B. Marriage in view of the fall

The fall of man into sin and guilt gives us the only valid way of understanding all the problems which now beset marriage.

1. Sin disrupted man's relationship with other people in every area of life. Thus Jesus in Matthew 19 traces divorce to the sinful nature of man. He carefully pointed out that although divorce "is," it is not what "ought" to be, for it was not in the beginning at the creation.

2. All marital problems are rooted in either sin or the effects of sin. It is not "human" to fight or to be selfish. Some marriages reflect hell instead of heaven because the ones involved in the marriage are unredeemed sinners. The institution of marriage is not at fault.

3. Part of the divine curse upon man was that the woman's "desire shall be unto her husband and he shall rule over you" (Gen. 3:16). A careful study of the Hebrew text reveals that the KJV mistranslated the passage. A better translation would show that the curse was that the woman would try to dominate the man and that the man would tyrannize the woman. This is evident by examining the parallel construction in Genesis 4:7 where sin's "desire" is to dominate Cain.

C. Marriage in view of redemption

Personal salvation through faith in the Lord Jesus Christ supplies us

34

with the only basis upon which we can restore marriage to what it "ought" to be, i.e., what it once was in the Garden of Eden.

1. Redemption does not negate the structure of marriage God originally set up in the Garden. Rather, it now gives the power and motivation to restore marriage to its original condition.
2. Since Christians are to marry "only in the Lord" (I Cor. 7:39), they must not marry non-Christians (II Cor. 6:14).
3. In God's plan of salvation, He set forth a redemptive pattern for marriage in Ephesians 5:22-23. The man is again established by redemption as the head of the family even as Christ is head of the church. The woman is to submit to the man as the church is to submit to the authority of Christ.
4. Since man is to view his relationship to his family in terms of Christ's relationship to the church, he must take upon himself the threefold office of prophet, priest, and king.

   As a prophet to his family he must teach them the truth and protect them from error. As a priest he is to lead them in the worship of God, teach them to pray to God and intercede before God on their behalf. As a king he is to provide for them, protect and guide them.
5. The key to successful marital life is the filling of the Holy Spirit since the apostle gives detailed exhortations concerning family living as examples of the way Spirit-filled Christians should live (Eph. 5:18–6:9).
6. In view of (1) the difficulties which are caused by the distress of persecution, (2) the shortness of life, (3) the nearness of Christ's return, and (4) the greater amount of work that a single person can do for Christ, the apostle Paul declares that God decrees that some of His people will be single all their days (I Cor. 7:7-9, 26-35). In view of God's plan of redemption, the single person has true dignity if he or she uses this freedom from the responsibilities of marriage to be more zealous and productive in the service of Christ.

35

SUMMARY

One of the greatest challenges which we face today is the development of a distinctive biblical world-and-life view. This Christian perspective needs to be developed in detail in every area of life, practical or academic. We are convinced that the whole counsel of God needs to be applied to the whole man in the entirety of life. Every square inch of this world must be claimed and conquered for Christ. It is to this end that this monograph is dedicated in the hope that it will stir up the minds of believers to fulfill their covenantal responsibility to obey the cultural mandate in whatever calling into which God has called them.

36

APPENDIX

In order to emphasize the importance of dealing with the hidden presuppositions which underlie the common objections to the gospel instead of spending fruitless time in dealing with surface objections, study the following chart. In this chart many of these common objections are traced to the real problem, the presupposition which is the root issue. Then a Christian answer is given. The chart is not to be viewed as something to memorize but rather as illustrations of how to trace surface objections to the hidden presuppositions.

SURFACE OBJECTIONS	PRESUPPOSITIONS	CHRISTIAN ANSWERS
"SCIENCE HAS DISPROVED THE BIBLE. I BELIEVE IN SCIENCE."	Science and scientists are "neutral" and "objective," with no prejudices or presuppositions. Scientific *theories* are always *based on facts*.	Science continually changes its theories according to the presuppositions of the culture in which it exists. Science is not "neutral," or "objective." The scientist is controlled by his presuppositions, as well as his world and life view. Scientists make mistakes and produce false theories. As a matter of historical record, scientific *facts* have never disproved one word of Scripture. The theories of various scientists may contradict Scripture, but there is no evidence against Scripture.
"CHRISTIANITY IS TOO NARROW"	The best religion is one which makes everyone happy and secure. It assures all that everything is "going to be all right." *No* religion should offend people by saying that it is the only *true* religion.	Logically, since all religions contradict each other, there are only two options open to us. Either they are *all* false, or there is only *one* true religion. If there is only one God, there will be only *one* religion. The person who objects is "too narrow." to accept the truth.
"I CAN'T BELIEVE A LOVING GOD WOULD SEND PEOPLE TO HELL!"	God is too good, and man is too good, for God to send man to hell. This person assumes that God thinks, feels, and acts as *man* does. "If *I* would not send people to hell, neither would God!"	God is not a man. Neither does God think, feel, or act as a man would. His ways and thoughts are above ours. The real problem is that this person wants a "god" created in his own image . . . a "god" he can live with comfortably, while sinning. God loves justice, holiness, and righteousness *so much* that He created hell. The love of God for His own nature, His law, His universe, and His people, makes hell a product of love as well as justice.
"IT DOESN'T MATTER WHAT YOU BELIEVE, AS LONG AS YOU ARE SINCERE."	Sincerity is more important than truth or morality.	This is not logically or morally defensible. No one can live according to this belief. Who would excuse sincere Satanists, who make human sacrifices? Was not Hitler sincere in his belief that all Jews should be exterminated? Sincerity cannot displace truth or morality; you can be sincerely *wrong*, and also *sincerely immoral!*

SURFACE OBJECTIONS	PRESUPPOSITIONS	CHRISTIAN ANSWERS
"JESUS WAS A GOOD MAN AND A GREAT TEACHER . . . THAT IS ALL HE WAS."	Jesus was a great human being. No one can deny this . . . *but He was not God* or the Christ.	This statement is self-refuting. If Jesus was a good man and a great teacher, then we must accept what He taught about Himself, . . . i.e., that He is God the Son, the Savior of the world. If He is not who He claimed to be, He was either a liar or a lunatic. If he was a liar or a lunatic, He was not a good man *or* a great teacher!
"MAN IS NOT EVIL, BUT GOOD."	People are basically good. It is their environment that makes them bad. Give them good education, housing, and jobs, and people will be good.	This statement does not correspond to reality. History and psychology give irrefutable proof that man is corrupt in his very nature. No one need teach children to lie, steal, cheat, etc. Hitler's Germany was the most highly educated country in the world. The Scriptures are verified by *all* data when it says, "The heart of man is deceitful and desperately wicked" (Jer. 17:9)
"CHRISTIANITY IS A PSY-CHOLOGICAL CRUTCH."	People accept Christianity because it meets some psychological need in them. Thus, it cannot be the true religion.	Christianity is shown to be true because it *does* meet all the needs of man, including his psychological needs. Since God created man, He knows what man needs. Thus, it is only logical to assume that the religion which God reveals will meet those needs. This position actually proves what it set out to refute.
"I'M AN ATHEIST. I DO NOT BELIEVE IN GOD."	They assume that they are competent to come to this position. They feel that there is no deity of any shape, size, or form.	The only person who can be an atheist is God Himself. To say dogmatically, "There is no God!" requires one to know all things, to be all places at the same time, and have all power. Thus, you would have to be omniscient, omnipresent, and omnipotent, . . . i.e., God! Atheism is a theological absurdity. It is self-refuting.
"IF CHRISTIANITY WORKS FOR YOU AND MAKES YOU FEEL GOOD, FINE . . . BUT DON'T BUG *ME* WITH IT!"	Everyone should do their "thing." As long as they don't bother others, it's okay. Truth and morality are not important. Only the individual pursuit of pleasure is right!	This is crude selfishness. The Christian's task *is* to "bug" others! Hedonistic lifestyles have always led to disaster. Just because something "feels good" does not make it right. Psychotic killers "feel good" as they murder their victims! This position is unlivable.

SURFACE OBJECTIONS	PRESUPPOSITIONS	CHRISTIAN ANSWERS
"CHRISTIANITY IS NOT RELEVANT."	It is not relevant to *me* in *my* life. It is not practical; . . . it's "pie in the sky, by and by."	True Christianity is relevant and practical. The Bible is concerned with *all* of life, and not just with "*soul saving*." This person has been exposed to defective forms of Christianity.
"WE ARE ALL A PART OF GOD. WE ARE ALL CHILDREN OF GOD."	This person assumes that "ultimate reality is of one being, and that man is part of this "world soul," or "cosmic force." It ends up in *pantheism* (all is God, God is all), or "paneverythingism" (all is Mind/Energy; Mind/Energy is all).	We are not a part of God. "God" is the personal, infinite Being who created this universe, not out of His own essence or being, but *out of nothing*. The Creator is qualitatively and quantitatively distinct from the creation. Pantheism and "Paneverythingism" lead to loss of identity and despair.
"I TRY TO KEEP THE GOLDEN RULE. I DON'T KICK MY NEIGHBOR WHEN HE IS DOWN. I DO THE BEST I CAN."	This statement is based on the assumption that God's acceptance of us depends on our person and performance. God will grade "on a curve" on the Judgment Day. If your good deeds outweigh your bad deeds, you will be all right!	God accepts sinners on the basis of the person and performance of Christ. Christianity is the only religion with a substitutionary atonement. We can never *work* our way to heaven. There is no "scale" to measure our good and bad deeds, for either salvation or condemnation. Salvation is by *grace alone*, through faith alone, in Christ alone! (Eph. 2:8,9)
"BUT, CHRISTIANS ARE AGAINST SEX. WHAT'S WRONG WITH SEX? IT IS NATURAL, SO IT IS RIGHT!"	They assume: What is, is normal. What is normal, is right. THEREFORE, what is, is *right*. Also . . . "If it feels good, *do it*."	The fall of man into sin and guilt has made man subnormal, and the world abnormal. What is, is *not* normal. We have desires which are *natural* to our fallen nature, but not *normal* to human nature as it was originally created. Sex is not wrong if it is "normal," i.e., if it is practiced where and when God originally planned.
"I TRIED CHRISTIANITY ONCE, AND IT DIDN'T WORK FOR ME."	Christianity is an emotional "high" which does not last. There is no "real" conversion experience. Because their conversion was false, *all* are false. They judge everyone else by their own experience.	It is possible to have a false conversion experience. Whatever they tried, it was not real! However, one false conversion does not make *all* conversions false. This is not logically defensible, and does not correspond to reality.

SURFACE OBJECTIONS	PRESUPPOSITIONS	CHRISTIAN ANSWERS
"I AM NOT A SINNER."	A "sinner" is a social outcast . . . a whore, a drunkard, etc. This person is self-righteous, upright, and morally respectable.	All people are sinners, though in various degrees. A "sinner" is one who has not done all he should, and who has done what he should not have done. Sin is true guilt before God. God demands 100% of us keeping 100% of the law, 100% of the time. Anything less is sin.
"I'M TOO EVIL FOR CHRISTIANITY. GOD WOULD NEVER ACCEPT ME."	Christianity is for good, respectable people, not for "sinners." God can never forgive really *bad* people.	According to the Bible, "good people" go to hell, and "bad" people go to heaven! Jesus said that He did not come to call *righteous* people, but *sinners*. Christianity holds out hope only for those who sense their unworthiness and sinfulness. To such, Christ says, "Come unto me!"
"I DON'T BELIEVE THAT JESUS ROSE FROM THE DEAD."	The universe is a closed system, controlled by the laws of nature, which are absolute and unbreakable. Since the resurrection of Christ is a miracle, it is *impossible*, since miracles *cannot* happen.	The universe is not "run" or "held together" by any so-called "laws." God is personally upholding and running the universe (Col. 1:17, Eph. 1:11). Miracles do not violate "laws," because "laws" are simply human observations of the ways God upholds the universe. Modern science now rejects the Newtonian mechanistic world and life view which lies behind the objection.
"I DON'T ACCEPT THE BIBLE."	Human autonomy . . . man starts *from* himself, *by* himself, *without* any outside special revelation. In that condition, man *can* understand himself and the world around him with all the interrelationships involved. This has always been the vain hope of the humanists.	The history of philosophy shows that human autonomy ends in total skepticism. If we start with man, we end in total confusion. Only as we start with God is the universe intelligible. The surface objection does not correspond with reality. (See Francis Schaeffer, *The God Who Is There*, Inter-Varsity Press.)

SURFACE OBJECTIONS	PRESUPPOSITIONS	CHRISTIAN ANSWERS
"EVERYTHING IS RELATIVE. THERE ARE NO ABSOLUTES."	Everything is relative to the speaker's mind/Man is the measure of all things. Might makes right. They assume that no moral judgments can be made on anyone for anything.	The above statement is self-refuting. To say, "Everything is relative," or, "There are no absolutes," is to give an absolute statement which is not to be taken in a relative way! The statement is also unlivable. Hitler and child rapists would have to be approved. No moral judgments could be given. But, all people make moral judgments. No one can escape this aspect of life.
"I CAN'T BELIEVE IN GOD. WHEN I SEE WHAT HITLER DID TO THE JEWS . . . AND SEE ALL THE PAIN AND SUFFERING IN THE WORLD, I CANNOT BELIEVE THERE IS A GOD."	We can make a moral condemnation of people, such as Hitler, without an absolute standard of morality and ethics. "God" is not necessary for making moral judgments.	The statement is not logically defensible. If there is no God, there is no absolute standard of morality, and no basis for "justice." The problem of evil requires the existence of God. It does not negate God. The statement is also unlivable. The existence of God is essential to discern evil, in order to condemn it. Without God, there is no "evil" or "good."
"EVOLUTION IS TRUE. WE CAN'T BELIEVE IN THE BIBLE ANYMORE."	Evolution is "fact" and not theory. All evidence supports it. There is no evidence to prove creation. All scientists believe in evolution. No intelligent person can disagree with evolution. It is the best rational explanation of the universe. Creation is only a belief, a superstition.	Evolution is a mixed bag of many different, conflicting theories. Evolutionary theories are theories put forth by some scientists. None of these theories stand up to a rigorous scientific or philosophical examination. Creation has the evidence, while evolution has only a dogmatic faith. See Shute, Flaws in the Theory of Evolution (Presbyterian & Reformed Publishing Co.), for a rigorous scientific refutation of evolutionary theories.
"THE CHURCH IS FULL OF HYPOCRITES."	Hypocrites receive God's blessings, and will go to heaven when they die. All Christians must be perfect! One slip, and they are hypocrites. There are no hypocrites in the bars, discos, or business world. The person giving the objection assumes that he/she is not a hypocrite.	All hypocrites are condemned by God, according to Matthew 23:13, 33. Isn't it better to put up with them in the church for a few years instead of spending eternity in hell with them? Christianity is a "sinner's religion." It is wrong to think that Christians have to be perfect. Besides, there are hypocrites in every organization and group within society. Look to Christ to become a Christian! Christians may fail you, but Christ never fails.

SURFACE OBJECTIONS	PRESUPPOSITIONS	CHRISTIAN ANSWERS
"ALL RELIGIONS ARE THE SAME. ALL ROADS LEAD TO GOD. THEY ALL WORSHIP THE SAME GOD. IT IS UNKIND TO SAY THAT CHRISTIANITY IS *THE* WAY TO GOD!"	They assume that if there is a God, He does not care what people think of Him, or how He should be worshiped. This "God" never revealed Himself to man, or made His will known. Also, they assume that all religions teach the same doctrines about "God," "Sin," "World," "Man," and "Salvation." If they *do* all teach the same things, Christianity is then only *one* way among many ways.	God has revealed His own nature, and how He is to be worshiped. Christianity stands unique and apart from all other religions by its doctrines. Each religion has its own "God" or "god." The Christian Bible, and the religion which flows from it, is the only way to God that *God* has revealed! Jesus Christ is the only way to God (John 14:6). It is not unkind to tell people the truth lovingly.
"CHRISTIANITY IS NOT RATIONAL OR LOGICAL."	Most people actually mean their *own* "common sense" when they use the words "logic," or "reason." They are victims of thinking that reality must be whatever they *think* it to be. If something is not "logical" to *them*, they assume it cannot exist.	If you begin with your *reason* or *common sense* as the absolute authority, you end in skepticism. Usually the people who make this objection have faulty views of Christianity: i.e., a straw man of their own making. The Christian system is in accord with the Law of Contradiction. (See G. Clark, *Religion, Reason, and Revelation* (Presbyterian & Reformed Publishing Co.), for a logical demonstration of Christianity.
"WHAT ABOUT THE HEATHEN?"	The heathen have never received any revelation from God. The heathen are not to be viewed or treated as sinners, because they are ignorant. They are "noble savages." We are "lost" when we reject Christianity . . . but since they don't know anything about it, they can't be "lost" for rejecting it.	The heathen are lost because they are sinners, who have transgressed the general revelation found in the conscience and in the creation. They are "without excuse" according to Romans 1:20, and under condemnation (Rom. 2:12). We are lost because of what we *are*, not because of what we *know*.

43

SUGGESTED BIBLIOGRAPHY

Preliminary Readings

Anderson, N. *A Lawyer among the Theologians*. Grand Rapids: Wm. B. Eerdmans Pub. Co., 1974.

Clark, G. *A Christian View of Men and Things*. Grand Rapids: Wm. B. Eerdmans Pub. Co., 1967.

———. *Religion, Reason, and Revelation*. Nutley, N.J.: The Craig Press, 1978.

Jones, D. Martyn Lloyd. *Truth Unchanged, Unchanging*. London: Evangelical Press, 1973.

Lewis, C. S. *Mere Christianity*. New York: Macmillan Co., 1966.

———. *Miracles*. New York: Macmillan Co., 1966.

McDowell, J. *Evidence That Demands a Verdict*. Campus Crusade for Christ, Inc., 1972.

Morey, R. A. *The Bible and Drug Abuse*. Nutley, N.J.: Presbyterian and Reformed, 1973.

Morris, L. *The Abolition of Religion*. Chicago: Inter-Varsity Press, 1964.

Orr, J. E. *Faith That Makes Sense*. Valley Forge: The Judson Press, 1962.

Ream, R. *A Christian Approach to Science and Science Teaching*. Nutley, N.J.: Presbyterian and Reformed, 1972.

Rushdoony, R. J. *By What Standard?* Philadelphia: Presbyterian and Reformed, 1965.

Schaeffer, F. A. *Genesis in Space and Time*. Downers Grove: Inter-Varsity Press, 1972.

———. *He Is There and Is Not Silent*. Wheaton: Tyndale House Pub., 1972.

———. *How Should We Then Live?* Old Tappan, N.J.: Fleming H. Revell Co., 1976.

———. *Whatever Happened to the Human Race?* Old Tappan, N.J.: Fleming H. Revell Co., 1979.

Short, R. *Why Believe?* London: Inter-Varsity Fellowship, 1962.

Sproul, R. C. *Objections Answered*. Glendale, Calif.: Regal Books, 1978.

————. *The Psychology of Atheism*. Minneapolis: Bethany Fellowship, 1974.

Van Til, C. *The Defense of the Faith*. Philadelphia: Presbyterian and Reformed, 1963.

Advanced Readings

Carnell, E. J. *Christian Commitment*. New York: Macmillan, 1957.

Clark, G. *The Philosophy of Science and Belief in God*. Nutley, N.J.: The Craig Press, 1969.

————. *Three Types of Religious Philosophy*. Nutley, N.J.: The Craig Press, 1973.

Geehan, E., ed. *Jerusalem and Athens*. Nutley, N.J.: Presbyterian and Reformed, 1971.

Lewis, G. R. *Testing Christianity's Truth Claims*. Chicago: Moody Press, 1976.

Lit-sen Chang. *Zen-Existentialism*. Nutley, N.J.: Presbyterian and Reformed, 1969.

McDowell, J. *More Evidence That Demands a Verdict*. Campus Crusade for Christ, Inc., 1975.

Morey, R. A. *The Dooyeweerdian Concept of the Word of God*. Nutley, N.J.: Presbyterian and Reformed, 1974.

————. *Reincarnation and Christianity*. Minneapolis: Bethany Fellowship, 1980.

Nash, R., ed. *The Philosophy of Gordon H. Clark*. Philadelphia: Presbyterian and Reformed, 1968.

North, G., ed. *Foundations of Christian Scholarship*. Vallecito, Calif.: Ross House Books, 1976.

Notaro, T. *Van Til and the Use of Evidence*. Phillipsburg, N.J.: Presbyterian and Reformed, 1980.

Ramm, B. *Protestant Christian Evidences*. Chicago: Moody Press, 1966.

————. *Varieties of Christian Apologetics*. Grand Rapids: Baker Book House, 1965.

Van Til, C. *A Christian Theory of Knowledge*. Nutley, N.J.: Presbyterian and Reformed, 1969.